B is for
BASKETBALL

An Alphabet book

A collaboration with the Students
and Teachers of School District No. 50
(Haida Gwaii)

ILLUSTRATED BY Judy Hilgemann
FOREWORD BY Robert Davidson
THE CREATORS OF *B is for Basketball*: Tawni
Davidson, Alison Gear, Joanne Yovanovich,
School District No. 50 (Haida Gwaii), and Beng
Favreau, Literacy Haida Gwaii.

mckellar & martin
PUBLISHING GROUP LTD
VANCOUVER, BRITISH COLUMBIA / HAIDA GWAII

with School District No. 50 (Haida Gwaii) and Literacy Haida Gwaii

AaBbCcDdEeFfGgHhIiJjKkLlMmNnOoPpQqR

For further information, contact McKellar & Martin
Publishing Group, Ltd., at 5256 Prince Edward Street,
Vancouver, BC, V5W 2X5. Please visit our website
at www.mckellarmartin.com.

12 13 14 15 16   7 6 5 4 3
THIRD EDITION

LIBRARY AND ARCHIVES CANADA
CATALOGUING IN PUBLICATION

B is for basketball / the teachers and students
of School District No. 50 (Haida Gwaii); illustrated
by Judy Hilgemann.

ISBN 978-0-9865767-9-9

   1. Basketball—Juvenile literature. 2. Basketball—
Tournaments—British Columbia—Prince Rupert—
Juvenile literature. 3. Alphabet books. I. Hilgemann, Judy
II. School District No. 50 (Haida Gwaii, B.C.)

GV885.1.b122 2011   j796.33309711'1   c2010-906970-6

Printed in China

Acknowledgements

We'd like to acknowledge the following students and teachers from School District No. 50 (Haida Gwaii) for their collaboration on *B is For Basketball*:

Ms. Cameron's Class, *Sk'aadgaa Naay Elementary*
Ms. Holmes-Saltzman's Class, *Tahayghen Elementary*, Ms. Perry's English Class, *Queen Charlotte Secondary*, plus

- Robert Davis
- Myron Edgars
- Olivia Favreau
- Jennifer Friesen
- Staas Guujaaw
- Larissa Howlett
- Wade Jones
- David McLean
- Taylor Moody
- Johnny Sharkey
- Jordan Stewart-Burton
- Josh Vandal
- Billy Yovanovich

- Aaron Edgars
- Emma Efford
- Thomas Favreau
- Mike Gravelle
- David Hill
- Annika Ingram
- Niko Kaminski
- Page Marrs
- Kelsey Pelton
- Captain Stewart-Burton
- Marni York

In addition to the students' involvement, *B is For Basketball* would not have been possible without the following people, each of whom played a significant role at various stages of the book's creation:

- Robert Davidson
- Tonya Martin
- Skidegate Band Council
- Richard Van Camp
- Janna Wilson
- Mike Woods

- Kathleen Gablemann
- Michelle Prouty
- Mike Tarr
- Linda Roberts
- Angus Wilson

In addition to many of the people listed above, the Illustrator would also like to thank:

- Jason Alsop
- Lee-Al Nelson
- James Hilgemann

Haawa to Kevin Borserio, Diane Brown and the Elders at the Skidegate Haida Immersion Program for providing us with a local translation:

- Jackie Casey
- Bea Harley
- Roy Jones
- Doreen Mearns
- Betty Richardson
- Ernie Wilson

- Golie Hans
- Grace Jones
- Laura Jormanainen
- Norman Price
- Gladys Vandal

Thanks also to Patricia Shields and Evan Sonkin for believing in this book.

We gratefully acknowledge financial support from the Northern Savings Credit Union, Gwaii Trust Society, and Literacy Haida Gwaii for the first edition of the book.

The Creators of B is For Basketball*: Tauni Davidson, Alison Gear, Joanne Yovanovich, School District No. 50 (Haida Gwaii), & Beng Favreau, Literacy Haida Gwaii*

History / Principal Funder's Note

It is not commonly known that the All Native Basketball Tournament began as an inter-village rivalry in 1960 with ten senior teams and five Intermediates. Since then, the tournament became very popular in a hurry!

The Tournament was originally male-only and was primarily focused on Pacific Northwest entries. There were teams from as far north as Alaska, and from as far south as Neah Bay, Washington, who participated. The men played in two divisions until 1993, when the committee decided to add the Women's and Masters' male divisions. This was a decision that doubled the size of the tournament.

In 2009, at the Tournament's 50th Anniversary, there were 64 teams in four divisions. The All Native Basketball Tournament was officially the largest Basketball tournament in British Columbia. The year 2011 is the All Native Tournament's 52nd Anniversary, and there will be 54 teams who will play for four championship banners. The First Nations People take great pride in the games and the Tournament has become an important annual event that is attended by many. What began as a simple sporting event, and has quickly become a very important social event, as well.

These days, the Tournament is about more than just basketball; it is a cultural event with traditional food, as well as drummers and dancers who open the games every year. We, as the Tournament's official committee, know how important it is to make sure that the Tournament continues to grow with each passing year.

PETER HAUGAN, President
All Native Basketball Tournament Committee

Northern Savings is proud to have been given the opportunity to support the *B is For Basketball* project. This children's alphabet book highlights the integral role that basketball has in Aboriginal communities in northern British Columbia, and is a wonderful, inspiring reflection of the uniqueness and beauty of our northern cultures and environments.

The brilliant text created by children of Haida Gwaii, Judy Hilgemann's exquisite illustrations, and the theme of the All Native Basketball Tournament are truly a recipe for its success as a book, and as a tool to engage in and enhance literacy.

BILL NICHOLLS, Interim CEO
Northern Savings Credit Union

NORTHERN SAVINGS
CREDIT UNION

Foreword

The All Native Basketball Tournament has been held in Prince Rupert, British Columbia for the past five decades, and the weeklong tournament has attracted many of the outlying communities to compete with each other on the basketball court. This tournament is about basketball, but there is also a great sense of family; it is a place to renew friendships, have reunions, or just to make new friends.

As each new ferry, airplane, and carload of players/spectators arrive from Haida Gwaii, Alaska, and many points north, south, and east of Prince Rupert, you can feel the excitement in the air. There is a sense of anticipation for the tournament, as well as the thrill of reuniting and visiting with family and friends.

Each year, many of the villages send their best players to compete for the cherished trophy — and the championship. But what does it take to be a champion?

Being a champion means making the team, making it to the tournament, and giving the game your best effort. Basketball is a great sport for learning the importance of team playing, good sportsmanship, and being prepared.

Being prepared means getting your body in good physical condition, and becoming a good shooter and dribbler by practicing shooting and dribbling. It's also important to develop good passing skills to become a better team player. Being prepared helps you to gain confidence, and that confidence will also make you a better player.

But don't forget: There is a fine line between confidence and over-confidence. The over-confident player is more likely to celebrate before the end of the tournament, thus weakening the likelihood of making the playoffs. The confident player will stay focused to the end of the game.

Be a good sportsman.
Be a good team player.
Become the champion that you were born to be.

Play ball.

Robert Davidson

Please have a look at each of the smaller illustrations in the sidebar of each page. Many items are found on Haida Gwaii and the surrounding areas and most are very important to the community as well as to the environment. If you'd like to learn more about Haida Gwaii, please go to www.gohaidagwaii.ca.

Aa

Aunties from Alaska arrive at the All Native Tournament.

ABALONE SHELL

Can you find the following things in the illustration that begin with the letter "A"?

Airplane

Apple

Auntie

Bb

The teams warm-up by bouncing the basketball.

Cc

The crowd claps as the captains walk onto the co

COPPER SHIELD

Can you find the following things in the illustration that begin with the letter "C"?

Camera

Cap

Clap

Cedar hat

Camouflage

Collar

Coat

Crowd

Chini (means "grandfather" in the Skidegate Haida language)

Chair

Cushion

Captain

Cane

Dd

Drums beat while the defence dribbles.

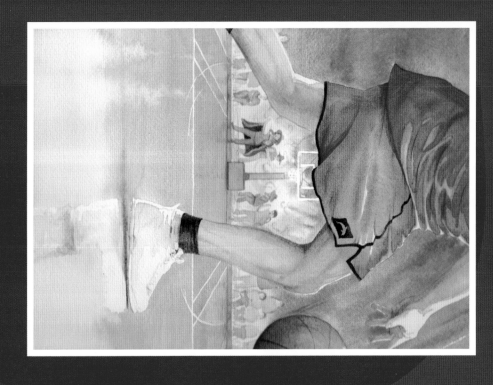

DRAGONFLY

Can you find the following things in the illustration that begin with the letter "D"?

Drums

Dancers

Dolphin

Ee

Everyone is energetic... and excited!

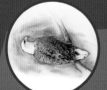

EAGLE

Can you find the following things in the illustration that begin with the letter "E"?

Earring

Eagle crest

Earth

Elbow

Eight

Elder

Ef

Fans feast on fresh fried bread.

FEATHER

Can you find the following things in the illustration that begin with the letter "F":

Flag

First-aid kit

Faucet

Fire extinguisher

Flowers

Frog crest

Foot

Fried bread

Gg
What a great game!

GREY WHALE

Can you find the following things in the illustration that begin with the letter "G"?

Gumboots

Girl

Gold

Glasses

"GO" banner

Green

Hh

Hannah hustles at half-time.

HERMIT CRAB

Can you find the following things in the illustration that begin with the letter "H"?

Hearts

Hoop

Hoodie

Hockey stick

Hat

Hair

Headband

Ii

*Ikes!** One of the players is injured.

* *Ikes* is an exclamation used on Haida Gwaii and the surrounding areas.

ISLAND

Can you find the following things in the illustration that begin with the letter "I"?

Ice-pack

Itch

Jj

Jo, who is wearing a red jersey, jumps for the shot.

JAM

Can you find the following things in the illustration that begin with the letter "J"?

Jogging suit

Jammed finger

Jersey

Kk

Kerry, from Kitamaat, is in the key to keep the ball in play.

KELP

Can you find the following things in the illustration that begin with the letter "K"?

Kiss

Khaki

L l

Larry leaps for a lay-up.

LONGHOUSE

Can you find the following things in the illustration that begin with the letter "L"?

Light
Lines
Laces
Lips
Legs

Mm

Mary mutters, "Matt please make this sho

Can you find the following things in the illustration that begin with the letter "M"?

Mittens

Mukluks

Mauve

Map

Moons

Man

Mustache

NECKLACE

Can you find the following things in the illustration that begin with the letter "N"?

Nine
Nose
Neck
Net

Oo "Out of bounds!" the official shouts.

OCTOPUS

Can you find the following things in the illustration that begin with the letter "O"?

Orca

Orange

Onlookers

Official

Pp

Pete passes the basketball to Percy.

PADDLE

Can you find the following things in the illustration that begin with the letter "P"?

Purple
Ponytail
Paramedic
Paper
People

Qq

"Quick! Try to make the shot!
It's the last quarter!"

QUILT

Can you find the following things in the illustration that begin with the letter "Q"?

Quarter

R r

Roy reaches for the rebound.

RAVEN

Can you find the
following things in the
illustration that begin
with the letter "R"?

Rainbow

Red

Running shoes

Raven crest

Ring

Read

Ss

The Saints slam dunk the ball in the last few seconds...

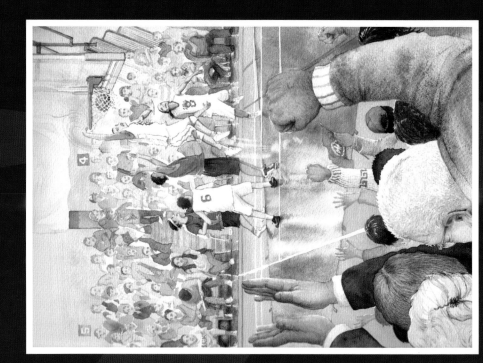

SALMONBERRY

Can you find the following things in the illustration that begin with the letter "S"?

Scarf

Spider

Stripes

Shoes

Socks

Six

Seats

Shorts

Stairs

Star

Sweater

SAINT

Shirt

Stripes

Tt

...and they win the Tournament Trophy!

*Can you find the
following things in the
illustration that begin
with the letter "T"?*

Tickets

Teeth

Tie

Ticket collector

Ten

Trophy

Uu

The uprising cheer is heard for miles around!

URCHIN

Can you find the following things in the illustration that begin with the letter "U"?:

Umbrella

V v

The Saints' entire village claims victory for their team.

VEST

Can you find the following things in the illustration that begin with the letter "V"?

Valentines

Vase

Violets

Vest

Ww

The final whistle blows. "We WON!"

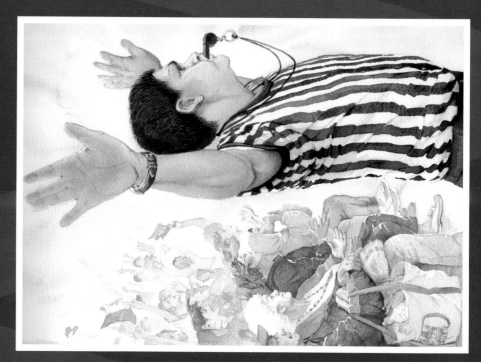

WOLF

Can you find the following things in the illustration that begin with the letter 'W'?:

Wool

Water bottle

Watch

Woman

Watchmen crest

Wave

Waistband

Whistle

White

Xx

Players exchange high-fives (and hope their injured player won't need an x-ray).

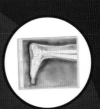

X-RAY

Can you find the following things in the illustration that begin with the letter "X"?

x-ray

Yy "YES!" yells their Chief.

YELLOW CEDAR

Can you find the following things in the illustration that begin with the letter "Y"?

Yarn
Yoke
Yellow

Zz

The winning team zigzags down the court.

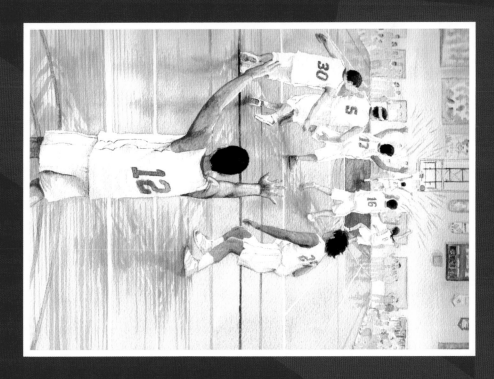

ZIPPER

Can you find the following things in the illustration that begin with the letter "Z"?

Zero

Zebra stripes

About the Authors and Illustrator

IN 2007, <u>KUUGIN KING NAAY</u>, an Aboriginal Children's Library, was established in Skidegate, British Columbia. When elders, educators, and families met to select books for their new library collection, a parent of three young children said, "We need a book about basketball!"

Basketball has been an integral part of life in northern British Columbia's Aboriginal communities for generations, culminating each year with the All Native Basketball Tournament in Prince Rupert, British Columbia. We believe children need books that reflect the world they see around them. After discovering that there were no books on Aboriginal basketball for young children, we decided to create one. Hidden within its pages are many more stories waiting to be told.

❧

Judy Hilgemann is an award-winning painter and illustrator from British Columbia. She has been drawing, painting, and telling stories with pictures for most of her life. She loves remote places and rugged landscapes where the light is clear and solitude is only a few steps away. Judy lives with her family in Queen Charlotte, Haida Gwaii. For more about Judy and her work, please visit: www.judyhilgemann.com

We hope you enjoy *B is For Basketball*.
—The Creators of *B is for Basketball*: Tawni Davidson, Alison Gear, Joanne Yovanovich, School District No. 50 (Haida Gwaii), and Beng Favreau, Literacy Haida Gwaii.

PUBLISHER/CEO Meghan Spong

PUBLISHER/EDITOR-IN-CHIEF Tonya Martin

ART DIRECTOR Mauve Pagé

AUTHORS A collaboration with the Students
and Teachers of School District No. 50 (Haida Gwaii)

ILLUSTRATOR Judy Hilgemann

PRINTED & BOUND Friesens

DISTRIBUTION Publishers Group Canada

STOCK 128gsm Matte Goldeast

FONTS Cartier Book is a Canadian typeface designed
and digitized by Rod MacDonald (2000), and based
on Carl Dair's original Cartier Roman (1966).

LOGO DESIGN Andrea Gifford

ABOUT MCKELLAR & MARTIN PUBLISHING
GROUP, LIMITED

McKellar & Martin is an independent, trade,
book publishing house located in Vancouver,
British Columbia.

We publish amazing authors whose books
are evocative, intelligent, honest, memorable,
multicultural, beautiful, and, well, fun.

We publish fiction, non-fiction, and poetry. We
publish books for kids, young adults, and adults.

Heck. We just try to publish really good books.

Please check out our list when you have the chance:
www.mckellarmartin.com. If you find a title that
seems cool, you might find something else on our
site that is worth a read. Or two. Or three. (You get
where we're going here, right? Awesome.)

Thanks for buying or borrowing or lending a book.
We really appreciate it.

McK & M